BOBCAT

BOBCAT

WRITTEN AND PHOTOGRAPHED BY

HOPE RYDEN

LYONS & BURFORD, PUBLISHERS

Printed in the United States of America
10   9   8   7   6   5   4   3   2   1

Library of Congress Cataloging-in-Publication Data
Ryden, Hope.
Bobcat / written and photographed by Hope Ryden.
p.   cm.
Originally published: New York : Putnam, © 1983.
Includes index.
Summary: Describes the habits and characteristics of the stubby
-tailed spotted wildcat that is native to North America.
ISBN 1-55821-143-8
1. Bobcat—Juvenile literature.   [1. Bobcat.]   I. Title.
[QL737.C23R9   1992]
599.74'428—dc20   91-43687   CIP   AC

BOBCAT

In North America there lives a wild cat that is rarely seen. It keeps out of sight by hiding in tall grass or rock piles or by climbing into the sheltering canopy of a leafy tree. It is most often active after dusk, when human beings are not about. Then it hunts mice and rabbits, stalking them on rubbery paws that ride soundlessly over every pebble and twig. During the daylight hours it keeps to the shadowy places, where its spotted coat blends with the surrounding vegetation.

This animal is called a bobcat and it is found nowhere else but on our continent. Africa has its cheetahs, India its lions, China can boast of snow leopards, but the bobcat is native to North America alone and it has lived here longer than man has walked the earth.

The bobcat is a lovely-looking creature. It stands tall on long legs and, though not much larger than a fox, it gives the impression of being a sizable animal. Its tufted ears ride high on a head set off by wide muttonchops. Its soft coat of tawny or gray fur is smartly marked with black spots and bars. Even the backside of a bobcat's ears are decorative. Each bears a conspicuous white dot on a black background. Without a doubt, however, a bobcat's most distinguishing feature is its stubby tail. It is likely the animal acquired its common name, "bobcat," because of its bobbed tail, which is rarely still. The bobcat's scientific name is *Lynx rufus*.

The bobcat did not always look exactly like it does today. When catlike animals first took shape many millions of years ago, even the planet did not look like it does now. By reading fossil remains, scientists have been able to reconstruct the history of the cat family, tracing it all the way back to a tiny insect-eater, or *insectivore*, that lived more than 70 million years ago during the age of the great dinosaurs.

This little bug-catching animal must have been very alert and secretive to have escaped the claws and jaws of the ferocious reptiles with which it coexisted. More than likely it spent a great deal of time hiding in treetops or under giant ferns, coming out to look for food only after darkness concealed it from view. When, however, the great dinosaurs mysteriously died out, this little shrew-like creature was more than ready to venture out into the open and experiment with a variety of life-styles.

Some of its descendants took to eating the plants that had formerly provided them cover. These early plant-eating mammals, or *herbivores*, over the course of long ages evolved into such modern-day species as the horse, the rabbit, the elephant and the deer.

Others of its descendants also made a change in their diets. These animals began preying on the newly risen herbivores. These meat-eating animals, or *carnivores*, over long ages evolved into such modern-day species as the civet, the hyena, the wolf and the bobcat.

Still other descendants of that remarkable parent to the entire kingdom of mammals hardly altered their life-style at all. One line remained in the treetops, and continued to feed on insects, as it does to this day. As a result, it is possible to gain a fair idea of what the common ancestor of the bobcat, the bat, the monkey, the horse, the seal, even man may have looked like, by examining the common tree shrew of Asia.

Of course, evolution proceeds at a mighty slow pace. Even when the first, most primitive sort of catlike animal began to take shape some 40 million years ago, it must have looked quite unlike a bobcat or any other of the *felines* we know today. Nevertheless, fossilized bones of this animal tell us that it already possessed a number of traits in common with today's cats. For one thing it walked on its tiptoes rather than on the flats of its feet. Animals that walk on their toes, such as the bobcat, the wolf and the horse, are said to be *digitigrade*. By contrast, animals that walk on the soles of their feet, such as the bear, the ape and man, are de-

Asiatic tree shrew

11

Digitigrade foot

Plantigrade foot

Canine teeth

scribed as being *plantigrade*. This first cat also possessed the four long, sharp canine teeth needed by cats to kill prey.

During the long stretch of time it has taken the earth to make millions of trips around the sun, all manner of descendants of this earliest cat have been affected and shaped by planetary changes. The world's climate has repeatedly warmed and cooled, causing countless species of plants and animals to appear and disappear from the face of the earth. The great land mass that once included North America, Greenland and Europe, and which had already begun to drift apart, lost all connecting land bridges. As a result each continent was isolated; each carried away its own special cargo of animals. Volcanic eruptions created mountain chains. Glaciers ebbed and flowed, covering and uncovering enormous areas and leaving lakes and rock rubble as evidence of their powerful activity.

Of course, these events did not take place rapidly. Conditions changed so slowly, in fact, that most animals had plenty of time to adapt to each new circumstance. Any unable to do so died out. Certain early models of cat, such as the saber-toothed tiger, for

13

*Fossilized remains
of saber-toothed tiger*

example, came into being and existed for many millions of years before becoming extinct. Scientists believe these animals sealed their own doom by becoming too specialized, too perfected for life in one kind of environment to adapt to continuing change.

Despite such losses, the cat family can be counted as one of Nature's successes. Not only does it predate the appearance of man by many millions of years, it has also given rise to a variety of species, forty-one of which have survived to the present. The bobcat's long lineage is impressive indeed.

No less remarkable than the evolution of a species is the development of a single animal. At birth a bobcat kitten is completely helpless. Yet within a few months it becomes a self-sufficient being, able to make its own way in the world.

A newborn kitten can neither see nor hear; only its nose is in working order. Like every infant *mammal*, it is entirely dependent on its mother, who nourishes it with milk produced in her mam-

14

mary glands. Without this food, and lacking maternal care, a baby bobcat would not live a single day.

Bobcat kittens are often born in caves or inside hollow logs or, if no better shelter can be found by an expectant mother cat, under dense vegetation. Whatever place she selects must be dry and concealed. To this *natal den* she carries mouthfuls of grass and weeds, which she rakes about with her claws until she has created a bed.

At a short distance from this den site, the pregnant bobcat then posts what might be described as "no trespassing" signs. Using her own waste material, she builds visible constructions—pyramids of stools. It seems evident that her purpose in doing this is to notify other bobcats to keep their distance; for while her litter is young, she must be able to hunt close to home and cannot allow the local supply of mice and rabbits to be used up by other cats. Throughout the rest of the year, the female bobcat will bury her stools in the manner of a fastidious house cat.

When bobcat kittens are about two weeks old, their eyes begin to open and their ears gradually unfold. Now, on occasion, the babies emerge from their dark den to play in the sunshine. At the first sign of anything strange, however, they quickly scamper back to the safety of their hidden shelter. This impulse to hide is important to their survival, for frequently they must be left unguarded while their mother is off hunting for food.

17

When sharp teeth begin to cut through their gums, the babies are ready to eat solid food. Now their mother has to step up her hunting efforts. Not only must she feed herself, she must also bring back rabbits and mice to her young. And catching large numbers of these creatures and dragging them across rough and broken ground and through tangles of vegetation is no easy task. Nor does the mother bobcat's work grow lighter with the passage of time. For as her kittens grow larger, so do their appetites. Because there is a limit to how many mouths even the hardest-working mother is able to hunt for and feed, bobcats do not give birth to large litters. Biologists have found that the average number of kittens born in a litter is around three. And most of these do not survive to adulthood. Perhaps if the bobcat mother were helped by her mate in the care and feeding of the young, as is the coyote mother, the species might bear and raise more offspring.

Male bobcats, however, play no part in the raising of kittens. They likely are not even aware of their offsprings' existence, for they live apart from their mates. Each adult bobcat, male and female alike, stakes out a good-sized land claim for itself and marks the boundaries of this territory with strong-smelling spray intended to persuade other bobcats to "keep out." By so spacing themselves, each animal assures itself a share of rabbits and rodents to prey upon. In some parts of the United States the average size of a single bobcat's territory measures eleven square miles. From this information it is easy to see why the species is never numerous, even though it does inhabit a wide range. Bobcats do not tolerate being crowded, and available space is parceled out among the fortunate few in sizable allotments.

The bobcat's desire to live alone, besides assuring it adequate food, serves the species in other ways. With distance between them, individual cats seldom have occasion to fight. Equipped as they are with fangs and claws to kill prey, these predatory felines would be vulnerable to attack from one another were it not for their solitary life-style. Thanks to their *avoidance behavior*, however, bobcats rarely meet. Even when one strays onto a neighbor's home range, the two animals steer clear of each other. The resident cat may even go into hiding until the trespasser departs. And the trespasser, without needing to be chased, will leave just as quickly as it picks up a whiff of the resident cat's spray. Thus showdowns between bobcats seldom occur; only when two animals meet by surprise, or during the mating season, when male bobcats ignore territorial boundaries to search for mates.

Every meat-eating species, be it wolf, eagle or bobcat, has evolved some such strategy to prevent it from destroying its kind. The wolf's solution to the danger inherent in being armed with fangs is exactly opposite to that of the solitary bobcat. Because wolves require one another's help to run down the large-sized caribou and moose they eat, they cannot live apart and avoid one another. Instead, they have evolved into highly sociable beings and form packs. Within this social order, each wolf knows his or her place, and fighting rarely breaks out. On the contrary, members form strong bonds of affection with one another. To strengthen these friendly feelings, wolves assemble at regular intervals to enjoy a group howl. Before breaking into song, all the animals express their excitement and pleasure in being together by wagging their tails and licking one another's muzzles. Even when a dispute does erupt between two members of a wolf pack, the

animals have invented a way to resolve their differences without resorting to bloodshed. The weaker wolf simply rolls onto its back and shows by its posture that it has accepted defeat in advance of actual combat. Seeing this, the more dominant wolf is appeased and the two quickly resume friendly relations. When an animal uses body language as a substitute for carrying out an action, it is said to be making a *display*.

Dogs and cats, being domestic relatives of the wolf and the bobcat, have retained certain behavioral patterns that tell much about their wild pasts. Like the sociable wolf, most dogs want and need a great deal of companionship and readily submit to the authority of a human being. As a result, a dog can be trained to cooperate with its owner in a variety of endeavors, just as wolves cooperate with other wolves in a hunt. Moreover, a sharp word from its owner is usually all that is needed to shame a dog into assuming a submissive posture, one that signifies the animal has accepted defeat in advance of actual combat.

By contrast, domestic cats are more solitary and do not readily submit to man's domination. When reprimanded, they do not crouch, but turn their backs. They refuse to perform useful work for others, for their wild ancestors walked and hunted alone and

did not develop team spirit. And, like their wild relatives, domestic cats often hide when a stranger enters their domain.

It is interesting to reflect on the fact that these contrasting social responses evolved to serve the same end. They are strategies which prevent the dog family and the cat family from shedding the blood of its kind.

Of course, a mother bobcat is not at all aloof in her conduct toward her own kittens. She is, in fact, a model parent, tenderly caring for her young until they are old enough to support themselves. Besides bringing them food, a mother bobcat cleans, protects and educates her babies. She is also most tolerant of their playful antics, allowing them to run across her body and play pounce with her twitching tail. Bobcat kittens remain with their mother until they are around nine months old and have grown to be almost as large as she is.

Their lessons begin early. Of necessity, little bobcats must begin to accompany their mother on short hunting trips when only a few weeks old. While the trailing kittens must certainly slow down the mother cat, nevertheless, having them in tow does spare her the difficulty of dragging cumbersome food, rabbits and rodents, across long distances to feed them.

Wild canines, wolves and coyotes, have overcome this particular problem in an inventive way. Wild canines leave their young first at a burrow and later in brush and tote food back to them until the pups are almost three months old. They do not, however, have to drag their catches along the ground as do wild cats; instead they swallow what they kill and carry it in their stomachs back to the burrow, where they are able to regurgitate it at the feet of their offspring.

The bobcat mother has not acquired this trick, so her kittens must become mobile at an early age. As soon as they are able, the family abandons the natal den and, thereafter, shifts about the mother cat's territory, camping but a few days in any one place before moving on to the next. This way, the bobcats give relief to the populations of rodents and rabbits they prey upon, allowing these creatures time to reproduce before circling back to hunt them again.

The kittens' long association with their mother is of great importance to their survival, for even after they have begun to hunt for themselves, they still lack skill at catching prey and need what extra food she continues to offer them. A mother bobcat also acts as a role model for her inexperienced young. By observing her, the kittens pick up clues on where to search for food. Just as important, they learn to recognize dangerous situations. The life of a predator is hazardous at best, and young bobcats have much to learn before they must set out to make their lone way in the world.

Even the act of killing must be learned. Though young kittens begin to stalk and pounce on one another almost as soon as they can stand, killing does not come easily to them. To make a kill, a young bobcat must first overcome its inborn reluctance to inflict a fatal bite. It is fortunate that bobcats possess this *inhibition*. Otherwise kittens might seriously hurt or destroy each other during wild bouts of play.

To help her young learn this difficult lesson, the mother bobcat presents them with live mice to play with when they are but a few weeks old. At first, the kittens do little more than prod this training prey with their oversized paws, just to watch it scurry about. They do not seem to understand what more is expected of them and, time after time, the mother cat may have to step in and show them how the act of execution should be performed. But even after being presented with the dead mouse, the kittens may still not grasp the lesson. They may even fail to make a connection between their former plaything and dinner. Using a distinctive sound, the mother cat will have to "tell" them to eat it.

Eventually, of course, one of the kittens will become so aroused by the darting mouse it is toying with that it will bite down hard

and discover, to its apparent surprise, that it has made a kill. That kitten is now ready to begin hunting in earnest.

Because most of the prey species the bobcat hunts are active at dusk or during the night, it is a good thing that a mother bobcat's earbacks are decorated with two white spots. In dim light her babies can keep these visible marks in sight. Another help to them is her stubby tail, which, when raised, reveals a white underside. Whenever the kittens fall too far behind, the mother cat will stop and call to them in a soft voice while waggling this visible flag.

Bobcats rarely mew like domestic cats, though they are capable of doing so. Normally, their vocalization consists of chortles and birdlike chirps. During mating season a bobcat will try to alert any prospective mates to its presence in an area by screaming.

Bobcats possess excellent vision and they are especially alert to movement, be it their mother's twitching tail, a fluttering feather or a creature scurrying through the grass. Even at night a bobcat is able to sight prey, for its elliptical pupils grow round and enlarge to admit whatever light does exist. Amplifying this low light are special cells in the bobcat's retina that act like mirrors. It is these light-capturing cells that cause a bobcat's eyes to shine in the dark.

Often a mother bobcat will park her young ones in a safe place along their travel route while she alone hunts for prey or stalks an animal too dangerous for her kittens to confront. A full-grown bobcat is capable of killing wild peccary or raccoon, animals that are capable of fending off a pack of dogs. But to overpower such fierce fighters, it must make use of the element of surprise. A bobcat is a master at ambushing victims from a hiding place and normally uses this strategy to bring down every kind of prey. For, despite lightning quickness, the cat family possesses little stamina and cannot run far before becoming winded. Therefore, a bobcat waits along a well-traveled animal trail to jump on passing prey or creeps up slowly on an inattentive victim, then seizes it in a sudden rush.

No animal is better able to play the waiting game than is the bobcat. Not only does it possess the patience needed to remain absolutely still for long periods, it is also wonderfully camouflaged by Nature. Even when out in the open, a spotted bobcat is surprisingly difficult to detect against sun-flecked vegetation or amid pocked rocks.

Bobcat eyeing wild peccary

As important to a bobcat's survival as its night vision, its patient nature and its camouflaged coat are its sharp claws. Without these tools, it could not escape up trees or capture prey, nor could it defend itself from attack. A bobcat maintains these vital weapons in first-rate condition by frequently honing them on tree trunks or fallen logs. When not in use, a cat's claws are kept withdrawn in protective sheaths of skin. For this reason, a bobcat's paw print rarely shows toenail marks and can easily be distinguished from the track of a coyote, whose claws are not *retractile*.

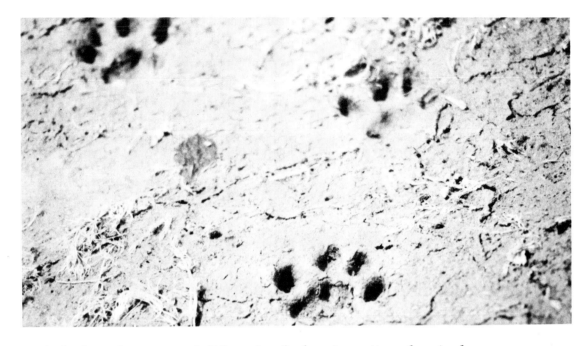

A bobcat's way of life—its behavior, its physical appearance, even its spotted ears—are the outcome of long ages of *evolution*, or *natural selection*. But how does evolution, or natural selection, operate to bring about so many useful transformations?

The process is often summed up by a single phrase: "the survival of the fittest." Yet it is easy to misunderstand this expression; some people even take it to mean that strong animals literally kill off their weaker relatives in savage battles. Nothing could be further from the truth. As has already been noted, bobcats would rather avoid one another than fight. In fact, any species that made it a practice to exterminate its own kind more than likely would bring about its own extinction. Certainly, such behavior could not be said to have *survival value* for a species. Obviously then, the phrase "the survival of the fittest" does not describe the triumph of combative animals over their more peaceable kin.

Nevertheless, in nonviolent ways, and without even being aware of the fact, individual members of a species are constantly pitted against one another. The best hunters, the best hiders, the best mothers, the most perfectly camouflaged, live long lives and so have time to bear many young. These superior animals pass their traits on to the next generation through heredity, and eventually their successful traits spread through an entire population. A better phrase to express this process of natural selection would be "the survival of the fittest *traits.*"

To illustrate how "fit traits" survive, let us suppose that long ago bobcats did not have spots. Then by chance a kitten was born whose coat was dappled. This characteristic would help to camouflage the animal and give it an advantage over its solid-coated relatives. Being better able to conceal itself from enemies, and better able to sneak up on prey, this spotted bobcat would enjoy a longer-than-average life span and so have time to produce more than the usual number of offspring. And because the young of this spotted cat would inherit their parents' coloration, they too would enjoy the same advantages—longer-than-average life spans and more than the usual number of descendants. In time, spotted bobcats would come to outnumber bobcats without spots. It is easy to see how a chance trait that offers an animal some advantage in life will in the end prevail and, over the course of time, come to mark an entire population. This process is called natural selection.

Not every new trait that arises by chance benefits the animal that possesses it. When a new trait occurs that confers no particular advantage on the individual so as to increase its life span or its ability to produce and raise young, that trait, or *mutation*, as it is called, usually dies out. Mutations occur all the time and are

caused by changes in an individual's *genetic material*—the blueprints that control physical development. These genetic changes may be brought about by exposure to natural radiation or chemicals or as a result of disease. Not every cause of mutations is known.

When changes are pronounced and spread rapidly through some isolated segment of a population, an entirely new species may arise that no longer resembles or breeds with its parent stock.

Jaguar

Mountain lion

This explains how, over the course of long ages, forty-one different species of cat have come into existence and occur in far-flung regions of the world.

Even in North America, seven species of wild felines exist, and until recently all seven could be found within the borders of the United States. Besides the bobcat, these species are: the jaguar, the mountain lion, the Canada lynx, the ocelot, the margay and the jaguarundi. Each one of these species differs from all the others in appearance and habits, and each plays a distinct and important role within a larger community of animals.

Canada lynx

Ocelot

Margay

Jaguarundi

The jaguar and the mountain lion, for example, are large and powerful cats. Some jaguars weigh as much as 250 pounds, and all adults are strong enough to kill a horse. Though the mountain lion is smaller than the jaguar, it too is a mighty hunter. Its favorite food is deer, but when pressed by hunger, it may even attack a 1,000-pound elk. The jaguarundi and the margay, by contrast, are pint-sized animals, hardly larger than a house cat. And the ocelot and the Canada lynx are similar in size to the bobcat, falling into a middle range of cats.

How has the bobcat managed to survive in the presence of larger and stronger versions of felines? How has this middle-sized member of the cat family managed to compete with the jaguar and

the mountain lion for food and living space? Conversely, how is it that the bobcat hasn't driven to extinction its smaller relatives—the margay and the jaguarundi? For that matter, how have three similar-sized cats—the bobcat, the ocelot and the Canada lynx—managed to coexist in North America?

Scientists explain that each species of North American cat has managed to survive alongside all the others because each has laid claim to a distinct *niche* in the environment. In simple language this means that each species has had to become a specialist at hunting particular foods not so favored by the others. Moreover, each species has sought places in which to live and breed that the others did not find particularly suitable.

To understand how various species have become adapted to different life-styles, it is useful to imagine life in the dim past when the earliest true cat roamed the earth. Perhaps some of the descendants of the first feline were, by chance, larger than others. These oversized cats likely were very successful at pursuing and killing large-sized prey. As a result, they ate well, lived longer, and produced many offspring who inherited and passed along the tendency to grow large. It is not hard to imagine how, over long ages, a line of big cats might have evolved.

But what of the smaller editions of the first true cat? Evidently even tiny cats found ways to make a living; otherwise they could not have persisted to the present day in the form of the margay or the jaguarundi.

Scientists explain that small cats also found niches to exploit. They took advantage of food sources not being used by larger, stronger felines. They also found places in which to live where they were safe. Some took to the trees. In the upper stories of a forest, a small cat could make a living stalking birds and tree shrews. Supported by fragile branches which would snap under the weight of a heavier animal, small cats laid claim to a food supply unavailable to animals the size of a jaguar or a mountain lion.

Today the descendants of these first tree-dwelling cats are best represented by the ten-pound margay, an animal perfectly adapted to life in its chosen niche. Even its ankle joints tell the story of its long stay in treetops. So flexible are they that the margay can run down a tree trunk headfirst, unlike a bobcat, which must make a backward descent in slides and stops as it alternately grips and releases its curved claws. For in order to support weight, a cat's hooked claws must be inserted right-way up into bark. The

simple trick the margay has learned is to twist its front feet half-way around and hang its claws in right-way up no matter which direction the rest of its body points.

So it is that a bobcat, while an able climber, is no match for a margay in a treetop. Nor can a bobcat compete with a mountain lion or a jaguar in bringing down large-sized animals, despite the fact that on occasion it can and does jump on and kill deer that have bedded down.

Nonetheless, the bobcat occupies its own special niche in the environment, and its particular adaptations to predatory life are no less wonderful than those of its fellow felines. Standing tall on rangy legs, it is ideally equipped to make flying leaps onto the backs of bounding victims. With such a long reach, it is expert at seizing small ground prey—animals that dart in unpredictable directions. As a result, the bobcat is able to catch and feed on all twelve species of rabbit and hare native to the lower forty-eight states.

46

Were it not for the fact that so many species of rabbit and hare inhabit so much of the North American landscape, the bobcat would not likely enjoy such a large range. Until recently, *Lynx rufus* could be found in every one of the lower forty-eight states, for it could fare as well on a diet of cottontails in the cool forests of Maine as on jackrabbit meat in the Texas sage. It could live on snowshoe hare in the mountains of Washington state or marsh rabbit in the Florida wetlands.

Cottontail

Jackrabbit

Snowshoe hare

Marsh rabbit

47

Dick Randall

Despite this everywhere-available rabbit supply, however, the bobcat may prove to be as vulnerable as all six other wild felines once native to our land. Four—the jaguar, the ocelot, the margay and the jaguarundi—are now thought to be extinct within our borders. The remaining two—the mountain lion and the Canada lynx—have been greatly reduced in number and today inhabit only a fraction of their former ranges. Though the bobcat has fared better than these fellow felines in America, its low reproductive rate, together with a fashion craze for its fur and the ongoing destruction of wild places, have caused it to disappear from wide belts of the Middle West and the East. Even in the Far West, where snowmobiles now allow trappers to pursue bobcats into once inaccessible haunts, the animal is on the decline.

The bobcat is especially vulnerable to the cruel leghold trap. Being curious by nature, it cannot resist investigating this terrible device—an instrument of torture that has been banned in fifty countries. In our own country, only Rhode Island prohibits the leghold trap altogether. A few other states restrict its use to particular situations.

It should come as no surprise to learn that bobcat populations from different parts of the country have evolved distinctive characteristics to help them cope with varying conditions. This may be reflected in their appearance. Texas bobcats (*Lynx rufus texensis*) are

Lynx rufus texensis

Lynx rufus floridensis

Lynx rufus rufus

the most vividly spotted. Florida bobcats (*Lynx rufus floridensis*) often lack ear tufts and sometimes are born with green rather than yellow eyes. Virginia bobcats (*Lynx rufus rufus*) are often reddish in color. Idaho bobcats (*Lynx rufus pallescens*) have long, dense hair. California bobcats (*Lynx rufus californicus*) are chunky in build. Arizona bobcats (*Lynx rufus baileyi*) have fur of medium length. And so forth.

Lynx rufus pallescens

Lynx rufus californicus

Lynx rufus baileyi

Canada lynx

Nine of the twelve subspecies of bobcat live in the United States and the remaining three are found in Mexico. Thus we may lay claim to the bobcat as being mainly native to our land. Although some bobcats from our northernmost states stray into Canada, for the most part the species has left that more wintry country to its first cousin, the Canada lynx, whose oversized paws better enable it to tread on top of deep snow. For on heavy drifts a bobcat becomes mired and is no more a match for the mop-footed lynx than it is the equal of a double-jointed margay in a treetop. So, despite the fact that both the bobcat and the Canada lynx are master hunters of the rabbit and hare, neither competes much with the other for this food. Each has staked out its own *geographical niche.*

Nor does that other middle-sized North American cat, the ocelot, challenge the bobcat's primacy here, for it is best adapted to live in a warmer, more tropical climate. The heart of its range lies south of the border in Mexico. That is not to say that there is no overlap between the ranges of the bobcat and the ocelot. Wherever the preferred climate of one cat grades into that of the other, both species may be found. Thus, bobcats occur in Mexico and until recent years ocelots were to be found in our Southwestern states. Generally speaking, however, each of these wild felines enjoys its own geographical niche, and as a result each is assured an adequate supply of ground prey.

Though the rabbit and the hare have long served as the bobcat's principal food, rodents of every kind, birds, fish, insects, even reptiles are also eaten by this *opportunistic* predator. On occasion an intrepid individual may even attack an adult raccoon or an isolated peccary or an unwary deer. And when times are hard, a bobcat may make a raid on some farmer's chicken coop. The bobcat must make use of every opportunity to satisfy its hunger, otherwise it might grow too weak to hunt for its preferred food. Opportunistic animals stand a better chance of survival than do those with fixed diets.

Nevertheless, it is the rabbit and the hare that have shaped the bobcat, have caused it to evolve its long legs. So important are these prey species to the bobcat that any decline in their populations is quickly followed by a drop in bobcat numbers. Thus the bobcat is held in check by the gentle creatures it eats as surely as rabbits and hares are held below a certain limit by the bobcats that prey upon them for food.

This is how it works:

Periodically, rabbits become extremely numerous—a situation that results in crowding, overgrazing and disease, and leads to a rabbit die-off. During the years that follow, while rabbits are scarce, the plants and grasses that nourish them are given a rest and so grow lush and thick again. At the same time, the rabbit scarcity creates hard times for bobcats. A mother bobcat may now have to travel such a distance to locate and catch an ample meal to feed her young that weakness and hunger drive her to eat what she finally does kill. Her waiting kittens go hungry and die. So bobcat numbers also decline.

As time passes, however, the cycle reverses. A decline in bobcat numbers is good for the rabbit population. With fewer bobcats around to prey upon them, and plenty of lush new growth to feed them, their numbers begin to build. This, of course, improves the bobcat's situation. Once again it finds a ready supply of rabbits to drag home to its young. So now bobcat populations continue to grow until crowding and disease trigger the next rabbit crash. Then the whole process is repeated.

This explanation of how rabbits and grasses and bobcats interact is just one example of how every form of life influences and controls all other forms of life in what are called *natural ecosystems*.

Each enjoys periods of rest, recovery, abundance and decline; yet no species ever becomes so prevalent that it is able to destroy its own food supply. Bobcats keep rabbits down; rabbit cycles keep bobcats down. Rabbits thin grasses; sparse grasses thin rabbits. The expression "the balance of nature" is often used to describe this interaction of life. A more accurate way to express this idea would be to say it is a "balancing of nature," for it is never static. No population remains fixed at any level for long. Each expands and contracts within certain limits created by the existence of all the others.

Man has not always understood the importance of allowing plants and animals to fluctuate in this way. When one species begins to peak, he often feels it is up to him to take charge of the situation. If, for example, he observes that rabbits have become extremely numerous, he may begin to slaughter them by whatever means are at hand. In so doing, he sometimes pollutes the environment with poison or bloodies his hands clubbing victims in cruel rabbit drives. Afterward, when the rabbit population drops of its own accord—as it inevitably will—he credits himself with the feat.

Even more irrational has been man's treatment of predators. Traditionally, he has regarded all meat-eaters as "bad animals," and in a misguided attempt to protect what he views to be the "good animals" (those he hunts), he has waged war against such valuable and beautiful creatures as the wolf, the grizzly bear and every form of wild feline. In so doing, he has undermined the functioning of many natural ecosystems and unknowingly brought harm to the very species he meant to protect.

Today we know that wild predators are important to the species

they kill. Besides holding their fluctuating numbers within certain limits, they also weed out the unfit and so maintain prey populations in sound condition. A hard-working predator, after all, cannot afford to squander energy chasing animals too swift and too alert to be caught. For this reason, wolves or coyotes will test possible victims and only make a serious run after ones that reveal weakness. Likewise, the bobcat, using a totally different strategy, is less likely to catch an alert animal than a dull-witted one that fails to notice it lying in ambush. Wherever wild predators are permitted to interact freely with their prey, they serve the species they kill by regularly removing the least fit—the diseased, the deformed, the less intelligent and the less alert. Thus they act as agents of natural selection; for it is the animals which escape their jaws and paws that remain to breed and pass their superior traits on to future generations.

So evolutionary forces have forged the predator to serve the prey, and the prey to serve the predator. Nor is the process finished. As long as man does not bring an unnatural and swift end to a species, it will continue to remake itself, meeting slowly changing conditions with ever-new responses. Just so, the bobcat, over long ages, has perfected itself even while it has served to perfect every other species with which it has interacted.

Those who think about this subject cannot fail to see animals from a new perspective. They will be less likely to oppress non-human forms of life and will understand that all life is of special value and has not been put on earth to serve man alone. They are bound to gain a profound appreciation of the natural laws that have brought each species, including man, to its present form.

Many people perceive these natural laws as the instrumentality through which God acts. However these forces are understood, it is important that we inform ourselves about them. For man has now acquired the unnatural power to destroy entire species at so swift a rate that the slow action of evolution is no longer a possible defense against extinction. It has taken the bobcat unimaginable stretches of time to stand up on its toes, to see in the dark, to dress itself in spotted coat. And what has taken 40 million years to be a bobcat, once destroyed, will never again walk soundlessly in the secret places of North America.

INDEX